Let Us Pray To The Lord

A **Collection of Prayers** from the
Eastern and Oriental Orthodox Traditions

Edited by Georges Lemopoulos

WCC Publications, Geneva

281.9

Cover design: Edwin Hassink
Cover photo: Peter Williams/WCC

Music typeset by Terry MacArthur

Icons 1, 5, 6 and 7 are reproduced, with permission, from *Olympias Nun Deisis: Selected Religious Paintings*, Patmos-Athens, H.C. Convent of the Annunciation M.B., 1989.
Icons 2, 3, 4 and 8 are reproduced, with permission, from Sirarpie Der Nersessian and Arpag Mekhitarian, *Miniatures arméniennes d'Ispahan*, Catholicossat arménien de la Grande Maison de Cilicie, Lebanon, 1986.

ISBN 2-8254-1188-4

Printed in Switzerland

Let Us Pray
To The Lord

Contents

Foreword

From time immemorial, in every human society with a religious consciousness, prayer has been given concrete expression in worship and ritual acts. It was therefore quite normal for Christians to appear as a praying and worshipping community from the very day of Pentecost. Even in times of hardships and persecutions they never failed to gather in order to devote themselves "to the apostles' teaching and fellowship, to the breaking of the bread and the prayers" (Acts 2:42).

Prayer is an act of faith, born of our necessity to meet the Triune God, to speak to a personal God and thus fulfil that intimate fellowship which consists of a communion between the Almighty and ourselves. It is prayer which lifts us into God's presence, giving us a sense of divine fellowship. It is by prayer indeed that we grow in this gracious relationship, in which we recognize God as our Father and discover that the divine will is our own peace. Prayer is therefore an essential part of our life and the key element which makes worship an act of offering to God.

Worship is a comprehensive activity. It embraces the whole range of human life and brings before God our achievements and failures, our needs and aspirations, our goods and ills. In other words, worship is an intimate communion of our soul with God in Christ Jesus, in the community of his church. At the same time it is an acknowledgment that our life is a divine gift and a reminder that in all circumstances, when we rejoice or suffer, when we sin or die, we always are in the hands of God.

But Christian worship is not a solitary undertaking. It has a communal and organic character. The worshipper, however lonely in appearance, comes before God as a member of a wider fellowship, the church. As the late Georges Florovsky once remarked, "personal prayer is possible in the context of the community, because nobody is Christian by himself, but only as a member of the Body". Even if we pray the Lord's prayer alone, we begin by addressing *our* Father, not simply *my* Father.

The World Council of Churches was founded nearly fifty years ago in order to enable churches to fight against such demonic forces as war, deprivation, loneliness and secularism, but principally to allow them to get to know each other and thus break down the walls of separation. According to its constitution, the WCC is a "fellowship" seeking to call its member churches "to the goal of visible unity in one faith and in one eucharistic fellowship expressed in worship and common life in Christ". And even if its members are still hindered by confessional barriers from their communion into the Body and Blood of Christ, they try nevertheless to affirm their uncompleted unity, conscious that where two or three are gathered in Christ's name, he is in the midst of them (Matt. 18:20).

In dealing with the question of "Worship and the Oneness of Christ's Church", the fourth world conference on Faith and Order (Montreal 1963) reminded us that "in Christian worship God comes to us in Christ through the Holy Spirit, sustains us through his grace, establishes us in fellowship with him and with one another, and empowers us for his service in the world".

By making worship a key element in the ecumenical movement, churches have manifested their intention to entrust their manifold activity in the hands of the Creator, the sustainer and giver of life, believing that a broken Christian community could not expect to become the undivided Body of Christ. They have done so in the conviction that without praying to God and interceding for the unity of divided Christendom, theological debates, convergence documents and agreed statements would remain meaningless intellectual exercises.

Those who are familiar with Orthodox liturgical life have surely noticed that in almost every worship service in this Christian tradition the first three intercessory prayers refer to those things we desire most: "the peace of God", "the salvation of our souls" and the "stability of the holy churches of God and the union of all". This is because in the midst of wars, hardships and social upheavals, the peace of God is our greatest longing and need; because the struggle for our salvation is a response to the Lord's sacrifice, for it was what Christ came to make available to humans; and finally because the intercession for church unity expresses our obedience to the will of the Lord who wished and prayer on the eve of his passion "that all may be one" (John 17:11).

It is noteworthy that after each of these three intercessory prayers of the celebrant, and indeed following every other petition for the acquisition of the spiritual and material benefits we require, people respond by asking for only one thing: mercy. *"Kyrie eleison* — Lord have mercy". As St Nicolas Cabasilas remarks in his *Commentary on the Divine Liturgy,* "to beg God's mercy is to ask for his kingdom, that kingdom which Christ promised to give to those who seek for it, assuring them that all things else of which they have need, will be unto them". It could be said therefore that worship is the living anticipation of the kingdom of God.

The present book contains a selection of prayers and intercessions from the riches of the centuries-old Eastern Orthodox and Oriental Orthodox liturgical traditions, developed through the ages in the East, the cradle of Christianity, in churches which — despite their different historical, ethnic and cultural backgrounds and the particularities of their theological "schools of thought" — were an integral part of the one undivided church, simply because they were professing the same faith and they were sharing the same sacraments.

For those unfamiliar with these traditions, the prayers collected here may sometimes sound obsolete and archaic, even those composed by contemporary saints and devout clergy or lay persons. Nevertheless, these prayers, full of theology and of biblical language and imagery, and touching on all aspects of human experience, are spontaneous expressions of the faithful who from the early days of the Christian era to the present day have never ceased to proclaim God's mystery, and to exalt the merciful Christ, who was incarnate for our salvation and died on the cross for the remission of our sins. They convey the message that God appeared in flesh so that humans may reach the state of *theosis* — deification — within a new world order, namely the kingdom of God on this earth.

Through this collection these prayers and meditations are offered to sisters and brothers whose theological and liturgical traditions are rooted in the "West", in an attempt to draw closer East and West, North and South, and thus to achieve a deeper understanding of one another.

As Metropolitan John (Zizioulas) of Pergamon has remarked, "the catholicity of the church is not simply a matter of bringing together existing cultures and nations, but principally a matter of uniting historical identities and traditions, so that they may be transcended in the unity of the Body of Christ". This being the case, it is obvious that the ecumenical movement will advance along the path towards authentic church renewal only by linking today's Christianity to the original sources.

If the immediate objective of our ecumenical search is the recovery of the apostolic tradition and the fullness of Christian vision and belief, then it is proper — and indeed imperative — to facilitate efforts on the part of the churches to rediscover their common roots in their common history and in the common apostolic tradition from which they all derive their existence.

The present collection of prayers makes a small but important contribution towards that end.

Georges Tsetsis
Permanent Representative of the Ecumenical Patriarch
World Council of Churches, Geneva

Introduction

This small booklet, a modest and certainly incomplete collection of prayers from the Eastern and Oriental Orthodox tradition, has its own story — a very simple story, which has unfolded during the last several years since I joined the staff of the World Council of Churches.

Prayer is a fundamental aspect of our work in the Ecumenical Centre; and I have often been invited, like most of my colleagues, to contribute to the preparation of a morning prayer, an opening worship for a meeting, a service of thanksgiving, an intercession on a special occasion. Each time I have been asked to do so, I have consulted various liturgical sources to discover an appropriate prayer that reflects the theological and spiritual treasure of the Eastern tradition. I have tried to identify a simple hymn which could either be used as a prayer or could be sung. I have sought whenever possible to illustrate an uninterrupted continuity in time, choosing prayers not only from the very early centuries but also from our own era. Finally, to denote the richness and multiplicity of sources, I have tried to include a variety of cultural expressions.

Several times colleagues and participants in our encounters expressed appreciation for the opportunity given to them to discover, albeit occasionally and partially, a spiritual matrix which has nurtured and strengthened generations of faithful through the centuries and across geographical, cultural, linguistic and other frontiers. Some wonderful theological discussions have been touched off by an expression used in a prayer which describes eloquently, though in the simplicity of the doxological language, a fundamental truth of our Christian faith.

What this shows is that the church is first and above all a worshipping community and that worship should also come first in our encounters as Christians. This is another way of affirming the common conviction that the *lex orandi* should have priority in the life of the churches and therefore in their common journey towards unity.

I was thus encouraged to share with a wider circle what I had collected. I recognize that what is brought together in these pages constitutes only a drop in the immense ocean of a liturgical and spiritual tradition which extends far beyond any frontier drawn by time or space. Yet after careful consideration, I concluded that there are at least three reasons to justify sharing this collection of prayers and hymns more widely.

First, despite its limitations this collection could encourage my Orthodox sisters and brothers participating in ecumenical encounters to make a similar effort and disclose in their turn the riches of the spiritual treasure of their own particular tradition. Indeed, there is in Orthodoxy as a whole an almost inexhaustible affluence of prayers which can inspire, enrich and strengthen the spiritual life and renewal of all who desire to live in the presence of the living God. Sharing them with sisters and brothers from other Christian traditions is an obligation we should take more seriously.

Second, by God's grace, we have reached a point at which Eastern and Oriental Orthodox theologians officially representing their respective churches can proclaim together the same Christological faith. This means that we are about to overcome one of the oldest divisions in Christ's Body, the church. And if Eastern and Oriental sisters and brothers are able to surmount difficulties and differences accumulated over the centuries, divided Christians of any other tradition can look to the future with trust and commit themselves to the cause of unity with renewed energies and hope. Significantly, Eastern and Oriental churches have felt the need to go beyond the agreements reached by theologians to address themselves to their faithful. They have decided to plan a series of publications explaining the nature and importance of the agreement, emphasizing the theological, spiritual and historical resources of the other, underlining the power of a dialogical approach, encouraging a common reading of history. Within the framework of such a broad effort, this simple collection, which includes prayers from both traditions, can perhaps offer its own modest contribution. Eastern and Oriental Orthodox speak the same language in worship and prayer. They have almost the same liturgical tradition. No doubt, this is solid ground on which to build together their full communion after such a long separation.

Third, a sharing attitude in prayer life seems to be particularly important because it defines the character of ecumenical sharing. Ultimately, sharing is an opportunity not to show off intelligence or wealth, but rather to display a loving concern for each other's growth in Christ. Sharing in prayers manifests our willingness to let the light of Christ shine in our midst so that we may live as Christian sisters and brothers rather than criticize each other's shortcomings or bewail together society's ills. Sharing in prayer is the willingness to share our life with God and with one another for mutual spiritual, theological and pastoral uplift.

There are many ways in which one could use the prayers presented in this collection. They can certainly accompany sisters and brothers in their personal spiritual journey. They can be considered as a resource for worship services. They can inspire and facilitate theological discussions about the profound issue of liturgical language. Readers should feel free to make their choice according to their spiritual longings, their liturgical sensitivities and needs, or their theological debates. To facilitate their task I have tried to indicate the potential of an inclusive approach, highlighting the possibility of holding together a prayer, a hymn, a biblical text, a meditation and even a symbol. Again, I would underscore that this has only a representative and not an exhaustive character.

I conclude these few introductory remarks by gratefully acknowledging all the colleagues who accompanied me in this task from the very beginning and by expressing particular thanks to Fr Georges Tsetsis for his advice and encouragement, and to Terry MacArthur for his readiness to help me in many different ways — not least by preparing the musical selections for publication.

Georges Lemopoulos
Office of Church and Ecumenical Relations
World Council of Churches

To the Holy Trinity

Holy God, Holy Mighty, Holy Immortal,
have mercy on us.

Glory to the Father and the Son and the Holy Spirit,
now and forever and to the ages of ages. Amen.

All-holy Trinity, have mercy on us.
Lord, forgive our sins.
Master, pardon our transgressions.
Holy One, visit us and heal our infirmities
for your name's sake.

Lord, have mercy. Lord, have mercy. Lord, have mercy.

Daily prayer

I glorify the power of the Father,
I magnify the power of the Son,
and I sing a hymn of praise to the power of the Holy Spirit:
one Godhead,
Trinity indivisible, uncreated,
equal in essence and reigning forever.

Hymn of the Resurrection

O God, the most-holy and blessed Trinity, save me.
O God, do not pass over my praise in silence.
Listen to my supplication and do not forsake me,
O most-holy God.
Through your Word and your Spirit, sanctify me.

Through your Word reform me,
and through your Spirit direct me.
Let your Word animate my dead mind
and your most-holy Spirit my will.

> Excerpt from a prayer to the Holy Trinity,
> St John Chrysostom, 4th century

We have known you;
we have loved you;
we worship you, the Triune God.
To you we pray,
upon you rest all our hopes of salvation.
Have mercy on us according to your great mercy,
and save us in your heavenly kingdom.

> Excerpt from a prayer to the Holy Trinity,
> St John Chrysostom, 4th century

O Light!
Divine and one Holy Trinity,
we who are born of the earth
glorify you always together with the heavenly hosts.
At the rising of the morning light
shine forth upon our souls your intelligible light.

> Matins Hymn, Armenian Sunrise Office

The poor and the needy will praise you, O Lord.
Glory to the Father,
glory to the Son,
glory to the Holy Spirit, who spoke through the prophets.
God is my hope,
Christ is my refuge,
the Holy Spirit is my shelter.

> Excerpt from a prayer,
> St Auxentios, 3rd century

We, your servants, offer you, O God, prayers and intercessions
on behalf of the peace of the churches
and the tranquillity of the monasteries;
keep your ministers in righteousness,
forgive sinners who turn to you,
make the rich rich in almsgiving,
provide for the poor,
support the widows,
educate the orphans,
sustain the aged,
guard the youth by your cross,
gather the dispersed,
convert those in error;
and let our prayers and intercessions prevail with you,
and we will offer praise and honour
to your high Trinity, now and always and forever. Amen.

Morning prayer, Syrian liturgy

With faith I confess and worship you, indivisible light,
the united holy Trinity and one Godhead,
creator of light and dispeller of darkness;
drive away from my soul the darkness of sin and ignorance,
and enlighten my mind at this hour,
so that I may offer to you acceptable prayers,
and obtain from you the fulfillment of my desires.
Have mercy upon your creatures
and upon me, a great sinner.

Excerpt from the prayer "Faithfully I confess",
St Nerses Shnorhali, 12th century

Glory to God in the highest,
and on earth peace, good will among all.
We praise you, we bless you,
we worship you, we glorify you,
we give thanks to you for your great glory.
O Lord king, heavenly God, Father Almighty,
O Lord, the only begotten Son, Jesus Christ, and Holy Spirit!

O Lord God, Lamb of God,
Son of the Father, who takes away the sin of the world,
have mercy on us.
You take away the sins of the world.
Receive our prayer,
you who sit at the right hand of the Father,
and have mercy on us.
For you alone are holy, You alone are the Lord, Jesus Christ,
in the glory of God the Father. Amen.
Each day I will bless you and praise your name forever.

Excerpt from the Great Doxology

Meditation: The Great Doxology

The Great Doxology is sung by all, for the mystery was revealed to the whole world and not to the shepherds only, but to all the nations as well. Therefore we say: "We praise you, we bless you, we worship you, we glorify you, we thank you for your great glory", because heaven is full of God's glory and so is earth. Whose glory? — that of God in Trinity. Thus the church speaks theologically in crying: "O Lord king, heavenly God, Father Almighty; O Lord, the only begotten Son, Jesus Christ, and Holy Spirit." See that it has preached the three persons in one divinity; in saying "we praise you" it manifests the unity of God who is on high, while by the number it proclaims the persons. Then we solemnly praise the incarnation of God, chanting: "O Lord God, Lamb of God" — taking this from Isaiah and the Forerunner because of his passion and sacrifice; "Son of the Father" — from the gospel; "who takes away the sin of the world..., you who take away the sin of the world, receive our prayer" — this is also from Isaiah; "you who sit at the right of the Father, and have mercy upon us" — this gleaned from the gospel; "receive" and "have mercy" — from David; "for you alone are holy, you alone are the Lord, Jesus Christ, in the glory of God the Father. Amen" — from Paul; "every day I will praise you..." — from the divine David.

Treatise on Prayer,
St Symeon of Thessaloniki, 15th century

1. The Holy Trinity (the hospitality of Abraham).

The Doxology   Greece

3. Προσ – δε – ξαι την   δε – η – σιν η – μῶν   ο κα –
3. Pros - the - xe tin   the - i - sin i - mon   o ka -
3. Lord   ac - cept our   prayer. You who

θη – με – νος   δε – ξι – α   του Πατ – ρος
thi - me - nos en   the - xi - a   tu Pat - ros
sit   at   the   Fa - ther's right   hand

και ε – λε – η – σον η – μας.   4. Ευ – λο – γη – τος ει
ke e - le - i - son i - mas.   4. Ev - lo - gi - tos i
and have mer -   cy on us.   4. O bless - ed   are

Κυ – ρι – ε   δι – δα – ξον   με   τα   δι – και –
Ki - ri - e   thi - tha - xon   me   ta   thi - ke -
You   Lord teach   me, Your stat - utes

ω   –   μα   –   τα   Σου.
o -   ma - ta   Su.
teach   me   O   Lord.

5. Πα – ρα – τει – νον το ε – λε – ος Σου
5. Pa - ra - ti - non to e - le - os Su
5. Ex - tend O Lord,   Your mer - cy

τοις   γι – νω – σκου – σε   Σε
tis   gi - no - sku - si   Se
un - to those who   know   You

λε - η - σον η - μας.
le - i - son i - mas.
mer - cy on us.

Romania

Sfin - te Dum - ne - ze - u - le, Sfin - te ta - ra,

Sfin-te far' de moar - te, mi lu - ies-te-ne pe - noi.

Holy God, Holy Mighty, Holy Immortal: have mercy on us.

To God the Father

I bless you, O Lord,
that you have worked wondrous mercies upon me, a sinner,
and have been most loving to me in all things:
nurse and governor,
guardian and helper,
refuge and saviour,
protector of both soul and body.
I bless you, O Lord,
for you have granted me the power to repent from my sins
and have shown to me myriad occasions
to return from my malice.
For you have mercy and save us, O God,
and to you we send up glory, thanksgiving and worship,
together with your only-begotten Son,
and your all-holy, good and life-creating Spirit,
now and ever and unto ages of ages. Amen.

Excerpt from a prayer
to the Almighty God and Father who loves humankind,
St Basil the Great, 4th century

O Lord, the nurse of all, let us not die of starvation
because of our greediness and contempt
for our needy brothers and sisters.
Therefore, fountain of goodness,
send upon the earth peaceful and seasonable rains
to bring forth fruit for our nourishment.
Ocean of compassion, cease the drought and the barrenness
which distress and afflict us.

Mingle together with the warmth of the sun
the dew of your kindness for us and your beasts.
Do not neglect us because we neglect your commandments,
nor turn your face away from us and shut your ears against us
because we disobey your ordinances.
For you are a God of mercy, compassion and love to humankind,
and to you, the Father who is without beginning,
we send glory,
together with your only-begotten Son
and your all-holy, good and life-creating Spirit,
now and ever and unto ages of ages. Amen.

> Excerpt from a prayer of confession,
> St Symeon of Thessaloniki, 15th century

Lord, bless those who praise you
and sanctify those who trust in you.
Save your people and bless your inheritance.
Protect the whole body of your church.
Sanctify those who love the beauty of your house.
Glorify them in return by your divine power,
and do not forsake us who hope in you.
Grant peace to your world,
to your churches, to the clergy,
to those in public service, and to all your people.
For every good and perfect gift is from above,
coming from you, the Father of lights.
To you we give glory, thanksgiving and worship,
to the Father and the Son and the Holy Spirit,
now and forever and to the ages of ages. Amen.

> Liturgy of St John Chrysostom

All-merciful Lord,
have mercy upon all those who believe in you,
my neighbours and strangers,
my acquaintances and those unknown to me,
the living and the dead;
grant also to my enemies and to those that despise me

forgiveness for the wrongs they have committed against me,
and turn them from evil thoughts which they cherish
in order that they become worthy of your compassion.
Have mercy upon your creatures and upon me a great sinner.

Excerpt from the prayer "Faithfully I confess",
St Nerses Shnorhali, 12th century

O you, beyond all
(is this not the only permissible praise
with which to address you?),
how can the word sing praise to you,
since no word can express you?
How can the mind perceive you,
since no mind can perceive you?
You are the only unutterable,
for all that is uttered comes from you.
You are the only unknowable,
for all that is conceived comes from you.
All beings — those who are endowed with speech
and those who are deprived of word —
proclaim you...
To you is raised a silent hymn
by all those who perceive your complexity.
For you alone everything exists,
to you all tend in a single block.
You are the end of all things.
You are one, you are all, and you are none.
You are not one, and you are not all.
O you who has all the names,
how shall I name you?
You the only unnameable.
What celestial mind can penetrate your veil
which is far beyond even the clouds?

Poems, St Gregory Nazianzus, 4th century

Psalm 136

1. Ren-dez té-moi-gna-ge au Sei-gneur   Il   est   bon
2. Ren-dez té-moi-gna-ge au Sei-gneur   des   sei-gneurs

Refrain

al-lé-lu-i-a   car   dans les   siè -   cles é-ter-
al-lé-lu-i-a

nels est   son   a -   mour   al-lé-lu-i-a.

3. A lui qui tout   seul   a fait pour   nous de   grand-es mer-

veil -   les   al-lé-lu-i-a   4. Il a   af-fer-

mi   la   terre   sur   les   eaux   al-lé-lu-i-a

1. O give thanks to the Lord, for he is good, alleluia.
   Refrain: For his steadfast love endures for ever, alleluia.
2. O give thanks to the Lord of lords, alleluia.
3. To him who alone does great wonders, alleluia.
4. To him who spread out the earth upon the waters, alleluia.

Meditation: Communion with God

Prayer should not be identified with petition or supplication. To pray does not mean "to ask", although it means always "to seek". There are levels and degrees. One begins with supplication and intercession, by articulating one's needs and deficiencies before God. Again, it is a prayer of beginners. Thanksgiving comes next. It is a higher level, but not the highest. It leads ultimately to the disinterested praise and adoration of God. When one comes face to face with God's unfathomable splendour and glory and praises God for his majesty, without even mentioning the benefits God bestows upon the world — then the human chorus joins that of the angels, who do not ask or even thank at all, but continually praise God: "Holy, Holy, Holy". Thus, in the Eastern tradition, prayer is ultimately theocentric. Eastern tradition admits no ultimate discrimination: it assumes an ultimate equality of all believers, clerical and lay; there is but one identical goal for all and everyone — the personal communion with God, through Jesus Christ, in the power of the Holy Spirit.

"The Elements of Liturgy", Fr Georges Florovsky

To Jesus Christ

Lord Jesus Christ, Son of God,
have mercy upon me, a sinner.

The Jesus Prayer or the Prayer of the Heart,
or the Perpetual Prayer

Christ, the true light,
who enlightens and sanctifies
    every person coming into the world,
let the light of your countenance shine upon us
    that we may see your unapproachable light;
and guide our steps in the way of your commandments,
    through the intercessions of your all-holy Mother
    and of all the saints. Amen.

Prayer for enlightenment

Christ, our God,
who has made it possible for us to pray together
and who promised that
when two or three are gathered in your name
you will give what they ask:
Fulfill now our request,
insofar as it is good and according to the special needs of each,
granting us in this world the knowledge of your truth
and in the world to come eternal life.
For you are a loving God
and to you we give glory,
to the Father and the Son and the Holy Spirit,
now and forever. Amen.

Adapted liturgy prayer

Christ our God,
at all times and in every hour,
you are worshipped and glorified in heaven and on earth.
Long in patience, great in mercy and compassion,
you love the righteous and show mercy to the sinners.
You call all to salvation
through the promise of good things to come.
Lord, receive our prayers at the present time.
Direct our lives according to your commandments.
Sanctify our souls.
Purify our bodies.
Set our minds aright.
Cleanse our thoughts,
and deliver us from all sorrow, evil and distress.
Surround us with your holy angels
    that, guarded and guided by their host,
we may arrive at the unity of the faith
    and the understanding of your ineffable glory.
For you are blessed to the ages of ages. Amen.

Great Compline

The Lord is everything to me.
    He is the strength of my heart,
    and the light of my mind.
He inclines my heart to everything good;
he strengthens it;
he also gives me good thoughts.
    He is my rest and my joy;
    he is my faith, hope and love.
He is my food and drink,
my raiment, my dwelling place.

Spiritual diary, St John of Kronstadt, 19th century

Grant, O Lord,
even to me, your unworthy servant,
your salvation.

Enlighten my mind
with the light of the understanding of your holy gospel,
my soul with the love of your cross,
my heart with the purity of your word,
my body with your passionless passion.
Preserve my thought in your humility,
and rouse me at the fit time to glorify you.
For you are glorified above all,
with your eternal Father
and the most Holy Spirit for evermore. Amen.

Excerpt from a prayer to Jesus Christ,
St Antioch, 5th century

Creation is now known to be free,
and they who were once in darkness
are now made sons and daughters of light.
Alone, the prince of darkness groans.
Let the inheritance of nations
that was previously in misery
now bless in eagerness
the author of this change.

Matins hymn, Holy Epiphany

Christ our God,
sun of righteousness,
by your divine touch
you gave light to the eyes of the blind man
who had been deprived of light since birth.
Enlighten also the eyes of our souls,
and make us sons and daughters of light
so that we cry out to you in faith:
great and beyond words is your compassion towards us!
Loving Lord, glory to you!

Vesper Hymn, Sunday of the Blind Man

Christ, our Lord,
you have abolished the curse of sin by your cross.
You have done away with the power of death by your burial.
You have illumined humanity by your resurrection.
Therefore we cry out to you:
glory to you, O Christ, our Lord and benefactor!

Resurrection hymn

What shall we give in return to the Lord for his gifts?
For us he became human
    and on account of our corrupted nature
    the Word became flesh and dwelt in our midst.
He was the benefactor to those who were ungrateful,
the liberator to those in bondage
and the sun of righteousness to those who dwell in darkness.
He who was incorrupt
ascended on the cross,
the light descended into hades,
the life suffered death,
and he was the resurrection for those who had fallen.
Let us sing to him: Our God, glory to you!

Resurrection matins hymn

Having beheld the resurrection of Christ,
let us worship the holy Lord Jesus, the only sinless one.
We venerate your cross, O Christ,
    and we praise and glorify your holy resurrection.
You are our God.
We know no other than you,
    and we call upon your name.
Come, all faithful,
let us venerate the holy resurrection of Christ.
For behold,
through the cross joy has come to all the world.
Blessing the Lord always, let us praise his resurrection.
For enduring the cross for us, he destroyed death by death.

Matins of resurrection

Yesterday I was crucified with him;
   today I am glorified with him.
Yesterday I died with him;
   today I am made alive in him.
Yesterday I was buried with him;
   today I am raised up with him.
Let us offer ourselves to him
   who suffered and rose again for us.
Let us become divine for his sake,
   since for us he became human.
He assumed the worse that he might give us the better.
He became poor that by his poverty we might become rich.
He accepted the form of a servant
   that we might win back our freedom.
He came down that we might be lifted up.
He was tempted that through him we might conquer.
He was dishonoured that he might glorify us.
He died that he might save us.
He ascended that he might draw to himself us,
   who were thrown down through the fall of sin.
Let us give all, offer all, to him
   who gave himself a ransom and reconciliation for us.
We needed an incarnate God, a God put to death,
   that we might live.
We were put to death together with him
   that we might be cleansed.
We rose again with him
   because we were put to death with him.
We were glorified with him
   because we rose again with him.
A few drops of blood
recreate the whole of creation!

          Easter oration, St Gregory the Theologian, 4th century

Eternal Son and Word of God, spring of healings,
you found the Samaritan woman by Jacob's well
and asked her for water.
What a wonder!
He who is enthroned upon the cherubim
speaks with a sinful woman.
He who has set the earth upon the waters
asks for water.
He who pours forth fountains of waters
asks her who was caught in the snares of the adversary
for water that he may draw her to him.
He who is merciful
seeks to give living water to her who is burning with sins.
Therefore let us praise him.
Loving Lord, glory to you!

Adapted vesper hymns,
Sunday of the Samaritan woman

Remember Lord,
    our fathers and mothers, our sisters and brothers
    who have fallen asleep
    in the hope of the resurrection to eternal life,
    and all those who ended this life in piety and faith.
Pardon their every transgression,
    committed voluntarily or involuntarily,
    in word, or deed, or thought.
Bestow on them and on us your kingdom.
Grant them the participation of your everlasting blessings,
    and the enjoyment of your endless life.
For you are the life, the resurrection and the peace
    of your departed servants, Christ our God,
and to you we give glory, together with your all-holy,
    good, and life-giving Spirit,
now and forever and to the ages of ages.
Amen.

Excerpt from a morning prayer,
St Basil the Great, 4th century

Let there be no gap between us and Christ.
For if there is any gap, immediately we perish.
For the building stands because it is cemented together.
Let us not then merely keep hold of Christ,
    but let us be cemented to him.
Let us cleave to him by our works.
He is the head, we are the body.
He is the foundation, we the building.
He is the vine, we the branches.
He is the bridegroom, we the bride.
He is the shepherd, we the sheep.
He is the way, we walk in it.
Again, we are the temple, he the indweller.
He is the only begotten, we the brothers and sisters.
He is the heir, we the heirs together with him.
He is the life, we the living.
He is the resurrection, we those who rise again.
He is the light, we the enlightened.

Homilies on First Corinthians,
St John Chrysostom, 4th century

Blessed are those who have eaten
    from the bread of love which is Jesus.
This is the wine that gladdens human heart.
This is the wine which the lustful have drunk
    and they have become chaste,
the sinners and they forgot the ways of unrighteousness,
the drunkards and they became fasters,
the rich and they became desirous of poverty,
the poor and they became rich in hope,
the sick and they became courageous,
the fools and they became wise.

Mystical Treatises, St Isaac the Syrian, 7th century

You have taken me captive with longing for you, O Christ,
And have transformed me with your divine love.
Burn up my sins with the fire of your Spirit
And count me worthy to take my fill of delight in you
So that, dancing with joy, I may magnify your two comings.

Pre-communion prayer

One is holy, one is Lord, Jesus Christ,
in the glory of God the Father. Amen.

2. *Women at the empty tomb.*

D. Soloviev: Russia

Be - fore the dawn, Ma - ry and the wo - men came and found the stone rolled a - way from the tomb.

They heard the an - gel - ic voice:

Why do you seek a - mong the dead as a man the one who is ev - er - last - ing light?

Be - hold the clothes in the grave.

Go, and pro - claim to the world:

The Lord is ris-en, he has slain death as he is the Son of God,

sav - ing the hu - man race.

Meditation: Luke 23:27-28,31

The men have condemned Jesus
but the women follow him weeping.
There are no women among the enemies of Jesus.
Expressing mocked motherhood,
they beat their breasts.
But Jesus says to them, "Do not weep.
Do not weep, Mother,
in three days I will rise again."

There is no need to weep for the priest
who is celebrating the sacrifice
of universal holiness.
We must weep over the destiny of humankind
over what humanity has made of its destiny.
Lazarus is dead, already he is decomposing,
already the enemies besiege the city,
the forces of nothingness besiege humanity
and drag it towards the empty abyss.
Jesus takes on this destiny to conquer it.
He raised Lazarus
and is preparing to take on the Divider
who has no hold over him.
So that one day he may eventually be able
to say to us:
"I wipe away every tear from your eyes;
death, crying, sorrow are no more
because the old world has disappeared."

Let us pray

The tower of Siloam still falls,
armies still set fires to cities.
It is not that you would punish us,
it is because we have become as dry wood.

You, the green wood, give us your sap,
so that we may know how to dry the tears
of the women of Jerusalem.

Make each of us a Veronica
who wipes the sweat from your face
so that your features on our icons —
and see how every human person is your icon —
may be for us the door to eternity.

Excerpt from the *Via Crucis*, 1994,
Ecumenical Patriarch Bartholomew

Orthodox

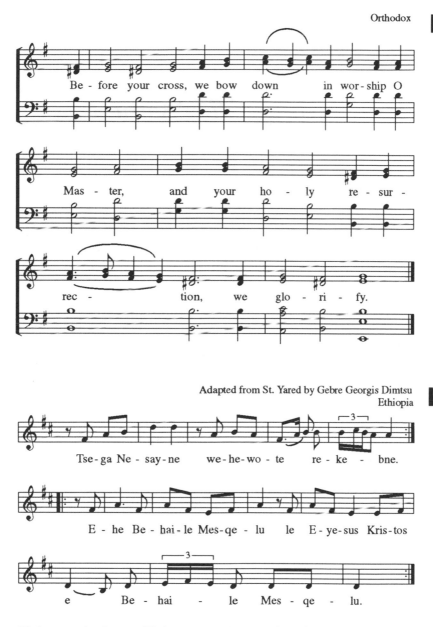

Be - fore your cross, we bow down in wor - ship O

Mas - ter, and your ho - ly re - sur -

rec - tion, we glo - ri - fy.

Adapted from St. Yared by Gebre Georgis Dimtsu
Ethiopia

Tse - ga Ne - say - ne we - he - wo - te re - ke - bne.

E - he Be - hai - le Mes - qe - lu le E - ye - sus Kris - tos

e Be - hai - le Mes - qe - lu.

We have received grace. We have received mercy, through the cross of
Jesus Christ.

To the Holy Spirit

O Heavenly King,
Comforter,
the Spirit of truth,
present in all places and filling all things;
treasury of good things and giver of life,
come and dwell in us
and purify us from every stain,
and of your goodness save our souls.

Prayer to the Holy Spirit

Let us celebrate Pentecost,
   the coming of the Spirit,
   the dawn of the promised age,
   the fulfillment of hope!
Behold how great and sacred is the mystery!
Therefore, we cry out to you,
Lord and Creator of all,
glory to you.

Vesper hymn, Sunday of Pentecost

The Holy Spirit taught the apostles
   to speak in many strange languages!
He also inspired the innocent children to sing:
   "Hosanna in the highest!
   Blessed is he that comes, the King of Israel!"

Vespers hymn, Palm Sunday

We confess you God, O Holy Spirit,
    and we bow down to you
    who causes us creatures to live
    and gives peace to the world.
You filled with manifold knowledge
    the ignorance of the disciples,
and being divided in the form of cloven tongues as of fire
    you manifested yourself to them
    through indescribable signs.
We therefore cry unto you,
    spare and save us, O Lord.

                    Hymn of Pentecost, Armenian liturgy

O Holy Spirit, how dear you are to the soul!
Paradise is the kingdom of the Holy Spirit.
O Holy Spirit, live in our souls,
that with one accord we may all glorify the Creator:
Father, Son and Holy Spirit.

                    On the Holy Spirit, Starets Silouan, 19-20th century

Come, O true light!
Come, O powerful one,
who always creates and recreates
and transforms by your will alone!
Come, O eternal joy!
Come, you who alone go to the lonely,
for as you see I am lonely!
Come, O breath and life!
Come, O my joy, my glory and my endless delight!
I thank you
that you have become one spirit with me,
without confusion, without mutation,
without transformation,
you, the God of all,
and that you have become everything for me.

I give you thanks that for me
you have become light that does not set and glory that does not
    decline,
and have nowhere to hide yourself.
No, you have never hidden yourself from anyone,
but we are the ones
who always hide from you,
by refusing to go to you;
but then, where would you hide,
you who find nowhere a place of repose?

Excerpt from a mystical prayer to the Holy Spirit,
St Symeon the New Theologian, 10th century

Prayer to the Holy Spirit   Russia

Tsa - rju   ni - bies - ni
O   hea - ven - ly   King,

u - ti - sii - te - lju   du - se   i - stii - ni
The com - for - ter   Spir - it   of   truth

i - ze viz - dii - e   si   i vsja is - pol - nja - ji
You that fill all   things,   and are in all pla - ces;

sa - kroo - vi - sje bla - giih
O trea - s'ry of good things

i ziiz - nji pa - da - te - lju
and giv - er of life,

pri - i - di i vsi - lii sja v ni
Come and cleanse us from ev' - ry stain.

i a - tsii - sti ni at vsja - ki - ja skvi - er - ni
And take up Your a - bode in us, O God

i spa - si Bla - ze duu - si na - a - sa.
And save our souls O Ho - ly One.

Milos Vesin: Serbia

O   Ho - ly   Spir - it,   come.   Make   us

feel   a   thirst and   hun - ger   for   u -   ni - ty.

Meditation: "Covenant... in the Spirit"
(2 Cor. 3:6) — the Church

The Holy Spirit is the very life of the body of Christ. He transforms the community of sinners into a "community of saints", into a koinonia in God and with God. In fact, the church is the fellowship of the Holy Spirit, the "covenant... in the Spirit" (2 Cor. 3:6), the instrument of renewal and liberation, and of the unity of humanity and the whole creation. It is by the Holy Spirit that the church is being sent to the world to accomplish God's purpose in human history and in creation. It is through the Holy Spirit that the church maintains its authenticity, continuity, infallibility and catholicity. The Holy Spirit constantly builds up the church, sustains and strengthens its life. The Holy Spirit safeguards the church's essential unity even in its brokenness and leads it into "all the truth" (John 16:13).

"Come, Holy Spirit, and dwell in us, purify, renew and sanctify us" is a common and almost daily prayer in Orthodox life.

"The Holy Spirit in Orthodox Pneumatology",
Catholicos Aram of Cilicia

3. Pentecost.

Beginnings

O Lord, keep us this day without sin.
Blessed are you, O Lord,
God of our fathers and mothers,
and your name is praised and glorified for ever. Amen.
Let your mercy come upon us, O Lord,
even as we have set our hope on you.
Blessed are you, O Lord,
teach me your statutes.
Blessed are you, O Master,
make me to understand your statutes.
Blessed are you, O Holy one,
enlighten me with your statutes.
Your mercy, O Lord, is for ever.
Do not overlook the works of your hands.
To you belongs praise;
to you is due song;
to you is due glory;
to the Father, and to the Son, and to the Holy Spirit
now and always, and to the ages of ages. Amen.

Matins

O Lord, grant me to greet the coming day in peace.
Help me in all things to rely upon your holy will.
In every hour of the day reveal your will to me.
Bless my dealings with all who surround me.
Teach me to treat all that comes to me throughout the day
    with peace of soul,

and with firm conviction that your will governs all.
In all my deeds and words guide my thoughts and feelings.
In unforeseen events let me not forget that all are sent by you.
Teach me to act firmly and wisely,
    without embittering and embarrassing others.
Give me the strength to bear the fatigue of the coming day
    with all that it shall bring.
Direct my will, teach me to pray,
    pray you yourself in me. Amen.

Prayer at the beginning of the day,
Metropolitan Philaret of Moscow, 19th century

In the evening, morning and noontime,
we praise you, we bless you,
we give thanks to you,
and we pray to you, O Master of all,
O Lord who loves humankind.
Guide our prayers aright
as an offering of sweet incense before you;
let not our heart incline to words or thoughts of wickedness,
but save us from all dangers
and from the evil powers that pursue our souls.
For to you, O Lord,
are our eyes directed,
and in you have we hoped.
Let us not be put to shame.
For to you belong all glory, honour and worship,
to the Father and to the Son and the Holy Spirit,
now and forever. Amen.

Liturgy of the Presanctified Gifts

Christ our God,
    your kingdom is an everlasting one
    and your lordship is over all.
You have made all things with wisdom
    and have established proper times and seasons
    for our lives.

We give thanks to you in all circumstances and for all things.
Lord,
bless the beginning of our church year with your goodness.
Grant that this liturgical year be for all of us a year of grace.
Make us worthy with purity of heart always to praise you.
Lord, glory to you!

Matins hymn, 1 September

Christ our Lord,
you provide the rains and fruitful seasons,
and hear the prayers of those who humbly seek you,
accept also our requests about our needs and concerns
and deliver us from worry, danger and sin.
Your mercies are as abundant as your works.
Bless all our activities,
direct our steps by your Holy Spirit,
and forgive our shortcomings.
Lord, bless the year with your goodness
and make it a year of grace for all of us. Amen.

Matins hymn, 1 September

From the East to the West,
from the North and the South,
all nations and peoples
bless the creator of creatures with a new blessing.
For he made the light of the sun rise today over the world.
O congregations of the righteous,
    who glorify the Holy Trinity in the morning of light,
praise the Christ, the morning of peace,
together with the Father and the Spirit;
    for he has made the light of his knowledge
    shine over us.

Matins hymn, Armenian Sunrise Office

We give you thanks, O Lord our God,
who by your visible light
have given joy to all your creatures,
and by the divine light of your commandments
have enlightened all who believe in you.
Strengthen us also, O Lord,
to keep your commandments in this day and at all times,
that having been enlightened in mind,
we may do your will
and receive your heavenly gifts with all your saints,
through the grace and mercy
of our Lord and Saviour Jesus Christ,
to whom be glory, dominion and honour,
now and forever and unto ages of ages. Amen.

Morning prayer, ancient Armenian prayer book

We bless you, O God, most high and Lord of mercy.
You are always doing great and inscrutable things with us,
　　glorious and wonderful, and without number.
You grant us sleep for rest from our infirmities,
　　and repose from the burdens of our much-toiling flesh.
We thank you, for you have not destroyed us with our sins,
　　but have continued to love us;
and though we were sunk in despair,
　　you have raised us up to glorify your power.
Therefore, we implore your incomparable goodness.
Enlighten the eyes of our understanding,
　　and raise up our minds
　　from the heavy sleep of indolence.
Open our mouth and fill it with your praise,
　　that we may be able without distraction
　　to sing and to confess that you are God,
　　glorified in all and by all,
the eternal Father, with your only begotten Son,
and your all holy, good and life-giving Spirit,
now and forever and to the ages of ages.
Amen.

Morning prayer, St Basil the Great, 4th century

Swahili

A - men.   Jē - na la Bwa - na   Lē hē-mē-dē - we

Tan - goō   Sa - sa   Ha - ta Mē - le - le.

Blessed be the name of the Lord.

Meditation: "Not to us, O Lord, but to your name give glory" (Ps. 115:1)

We may use God's name wrongfully in prayers when our minds are distracted with something else. Then the words of the Lord apply to us: "this people honours me with their lips, but their hearts are far from me" (Mark 7:6).

Are they not using God's name wrongfully of whom the Lord said, "not everyone who says to me, 'Lord, Lord,' will enter the kingdom of heaven," and those who will say to him, "Lord, Lord, did we not prophesy in your name, and cast out demons in your name?" (Matt. 7:22)? Are they not also using God's name wrongfully who begin their meetings with prayer, in the name of the Father and the Son and the Holy Spirit, then they quarrel in their discussions or speak improper words as if all their prayers were useless and the use of the Lord's name was in vain?

It is not proper to use the Lord's name with reverence only in prayers and worship, or when we are in the church. We ought to use God's name with solemnity on every occasion and everywhere. We ought to glorify and praise God's name all the time, as the Psalmist said, "Praise the name of the Lord. Blessed be the name of the Lord from this time and forevermore" (Ps. 113:1-2). Job the righteous said in his tribulations, "The Lord gave, and the Lord has taken away; blessed be the name of the Lord" (Job 1:21).

In any work we do, our objective should be the glorification of Lord's name saying, "Not to us, O Lord, but to your name give glory" (Ps. 115:1).

Meditations on the Ten Commandments, Pope Shenouda III

"Lord, Teach Us to Pray"
Luke 11:1

O Lord, Jesus Christ my God, forsake me not.
O Lord, do not stand afar off from me.
O Lord, stretch out to me a helping hand.
O Lord, support me with the fear of you.
O Lord, plant this fear and the love for you in my heart.
O Lord, teach me to do your will.

> Excerpt from a morning prayer,
> St Paisios the Great, 4th century

O Lord, as you command;
O Lord, as you know;
O Lord, as you wish,
so let your will be done in me.

> Prayer according to the cycle of the twenty-four hours,
> St John Chrysostom, 4th century

O Lord our God,
you have given your peace to the people
and sent down the gift of your all-Holy Spirit
to your disciples and apostles,
you have opened their lips
with your power of fiery tongues,
open also the lips of us sinners
and teach us how to pray and for whom to pray.
For you are blessed and glorified
in all your saints
to the ages of ages. Amen.

> Excerpt from a prayer,
> St Basil the Great, 4th century

Have mercy on me, O Lord.
Strengthen my soul;
govern the rest of my life towards your will,
as your compassion and love for humankind know best.

Excerpt from a prayer,
St Basil the Great, 4th century

As I rise up out of the dark,
O lover of humankind,
I beseech you,
enlighten and guide me also
in your commandments,
and teach me to always do your will.

Matins hymn, Sunday in Lent

Lord, we know not what to ask of you.
You alone know what our true needs are.
You love us more than we ourselves know how to love.
Help us to know our true needs
which may be hidden from us.
We dare not ask for either a cross or a consolation.
We can only wait upon you;
our hearts are open to you.
We offer ourselves to you as a living sacrifice.
We put all our trust in you.
We have no other desire than to fulfill your will.
Teach us to pray;
pray yourself in us. Amen.

Excerpt from a prayer,
Metropolitan Philaret of Moscow, 19th century

O Jesus, Word with infinite names,
show me what and how
I should ask from you in my requests.
O Jesus, Son of God, have mercy on me.

Excerpt from a prayer to our Lord Jesus Christ,
St Nicodemos of Mount Athos, 18th century

Meditation: Prayer — Some Quotations from the "Philocalia"

— Prayer is the ascent of the intellect to God.
— Pray first for the purification of the passions (that is, wrong desires); second, for deliverance from ignorance and forgetfulness; and third, for deliverance from all temptation, trial and dereliction.
— In your prayer, seek only righteousness and the kingdom of God, that is, virtue and spiritual knowledge; everything else "will be given to you" (Matt. 6:33).
— Do not pray for the fulfillment of your wishes, for they may not accord with the will of God. But pray as you have been taught, saying: thy will be done in me (cf. Luke 22:42). Always entreat him in this way — that his will be done. For God desires what is good and profitable for you, whereas you do not always ask for this.
— Whether you pray with brothers and sisters or alone, try to pray simply, not as a routine, but with conscious awareness of your prayer.
— Try not to pray against anyone in your prayer, so that you do not destroy what you are building and make your prayer loathsome.
— If you want to pray, do nothing that is opposed to prayer, so that God may draw near and be with you.

Confession of Sins — Repentance

O Lord and Master of my life,
take from me
    the spirit of sloth, despair, lust of power and idle talk.
But give rather
    the spirit of chastity, humility, patience,
    and love to your servant.
Yes, O Lord and King, grant to me to see my own sins,
    and not to judge my sisters and brothers,
for you are blessed unto ages of ages. Amen.

The Lenten prayer of St Ephraim the Syrian

Try me, O God, and discern my paths;
see if there is a way of transgression in me,
    and turn me away from it;
and lead me into the eternal way, O God,
you who have said,
"I am the way and the truth and the life,"
for you are blessed unto the ages. Amen.

Excerpt from a prayer,
St Macarius of Alexandria, 4th century

O Lord,
you who have measured
the heights and the earth
in the hollow of your hand,
and created the six-wing seraphim
to cry out to you with an unceasing voice

Holy, Holy, Holy,
glory to your name.
Deliver me
from the mouth of the evil one,
O Master!
Forget my many evil deeds
and through the multitude of your compassion
grant me daily forgiveness,
for you are blessed
unto the ages. Amen.

Saint Sarah, 4th century

O Jesus, the most-good goodness,
I have done no good before you;
but grant that I may make a beginning
because of your goodness.

Excerpt from a prayer to our Lord Jesus Christ,
St Nikodemos of the Holy Mountain, 18th century

At all times
we beseech the Lord who is merciful
to grant that we may love our enemies.
By the grace of God
we have experienced what the love of God is,
and what it is to love our neighbours;
day and night we pray to the Lord for love,
and the Lord gives us tears to weep for the whole world.
But if we find fault with any brother and sister
or look on them with an unkind eye
our tears dry up and our soul sinks into despondency.
Even so we begin again to entreat forgiveness of the Lord,
and the Lord in his mercy forgives us, sinners.

Starets Silouan, 19th-20th century

I, who am full of transgressions, judge those who transgress.
If I am insulted, I defend myself.

If I am not honoured, I feel abhorred
   and consider as enemies those who tell me the truth.
If I am not flattered, I feel disgusted.
Being unworthy, I except honours.
Those who do not serve me I defame as arrogant.
I ignore the brother and sister who are sick,
      but when I am sick,
      I want to be loved and cared for.
I despise the superiors and overlook the inferiors.
If I keep myself even for a little bit
      from unreasonable desires,
      I become vainglorious.
If I attain some degree of vigilance,
      I am entrapped by its opposite.
If I restrain myself from foods,
      I am thrown down because of my pride.
If I make some progress in virtue,
      I boast before my brothers and sisters.
Externally I appear humble,
      but in my soul I am presumptuous.
I am not going to mention the vain thoughts I have in church
      and the wanderings of my mind during prayer.
I leave aside the hypocritical meetings,
      the greed in the give and take of business,
      the publication of the mistakes of others
      and the disastrous slanders.
This is my accursed life.
O Lord, grant me repentance
for the sake of your infinite compassion.

Excerpt from a prayer to our Lord Jesus Christ,
St Ephraim the Syrian, 4th century

We claim no right;
no one can open the mouth to you.
Priests and people have declined all together,
shepherds and sheep have sinned also,
kings and people,
subjects and rulers,

rich and poor,
old and young,
and we have nothing to present as our intercession.
Only this we declare as ours,
that we know you our only God,
the Father of our Lord Jesus Christ,
your only-begotten Son who was incarnate for us,
and your all-holy Spirit.

Excerpt from a prayer of confession,
St Symeon of Thessaloniki, 14th/15th century

Look upon me in compassion, O God,
with your merciful eyes
and accept my fervent confession.
Have mercy on me, O God, have mercy on me.

Instead of freedom from possessions, O Saviour,
I have pursued a life in love with material things;
and now I bear a heavy burden.
Have mercy on me, O God, have mercy on me.

Lord, you love humankind and desire that all should be saved.
In your goodness call me back and accept me in repentance.
Have mercy on me, O God, have mercy on me.

Excerpt from the Second Canticle,
the Great Canon by St Andrew

Meditation: Luke 23:39-43

All our destiny is summed up
in that of the two thieves.
They are not strangers to us, they are ourselves,
our only choice is
between the one on the left and the one on the right.
The thief on the left
puts the final temptation to Jesus:
"If you are the Messiah then save yourself."
Already the priests and soldiers had said:

"let him save himself and we will believe in him."
But while Jesus remains silent, the other thief,
speaking to the first, says:
"We men, we kill and are killed in our turn,
death is deeply written into us.
But in Jesus, in whom there is no evil,
there is not this inevitability of death,
only death out of love."
And the criminal who is immobilized by the nails
holds on to the ultimate freedom, that of faith,
and cries out: "Jesus, remember me
when you come into your kingdom."
Had he sensed that the kingdom was no longer
in the future?
It is here, it is Jesus in his sacrifice of love.
It is here, it is Jesus, one Breath with the Father.
In him the world of sorrows becomes paradise.
And now, turning his eyes towards the thief,
he says to him:
"Today you will be with me in paradise."

Let us pray

Jesus, each of us is both the thief who blasphemes
and the one who believes.
I have faith, Lord, help my lack of faith.
I am nailed to death, there is nothing I can do
but cry out: "Jesus, remember me
when you come with your kingdom."

Jesus, I know nothing, I understand nothing
in this horrific world.
But you, you come to me, with open arms,
with open heart,
and your presence alone is my paradise.
Ah, remember me
when you come with your kingdom.

Glory and praise to you, you who welcome
not the healthy but the sick,
you whose unexpected friend is a criminal
cut off by the justice of men.
Already you are going down to hell and setting free
those who cry out to you:
"Remember us, Lord,
when you come with your kingdom."

Excerpt from the "Via Crucis", 1994,
Ecumenical Patriarch Bartholomew

4. Crucifixion, from a Bible dated 1330.

Before and After the
Gospel Reading

O Lord our God and Saviour,
who sent the disciples and apostles to the very ends of the earth
to teach and proclaim your message,
to heal all illnesses
and to reveal the mysteries of the faith
which have been hidden from humankind
since the creation of the earth,
send us your blessing and enlighten our understanding,
so that we may be given the gift of final perseverance.
May we be enabled to do and to act
in accordance with your commands
as set out in the gospel,
and may the fruit of the gospel
be increased in us many times over,
that we may obtain forgiveness of our sins
and so be considered worthy to obtain our heavenly reward.

Prayer from the Ethiopian liturgy

O Lord, who revealed the mystery of Christ's gospel
    through your holy apostles,
        according to the power of your grace
        that empowered them to go through the world
        and proclaim the good news of your mercy,
may we be made worthy to share with them.
May we always walk in their paths
and imitate them in their struggles.

Preserve your holy church, which you founded through them;
may the faithful be blessed
and may your church continue to increase,
through Jesus Christ, our Lord,
through whom honour, glory, power and worship
    are due to you,
with him and the Holy Spirit, the life-giver,
now and forevermore. Amen.

Prayer from the Coptic liturgy

O God of knowledge and wisdom,
you reveal all things that are hidden
and give the Word and his power
to all those who preach the gospel.
Of your goodness you called Paul, who had been a persecutor,
to become a chosen apostle
and preacher of the gospel of Christ, our God.
O God, lover of humankind,
we earnestly beg you
graciously to grant us and to all your people
minds free from distractions
and imbued with crystal-like lucidity,
so that we may learn and appreciate your holy teaching
which has come to us by him.
Just as he was made in your likeness,
may we be made like him in deed and firmness of doctrine,
so that we may praise your holy name
and glorify you in your cross.
You are the one to whom we offer praise, glory and worship;
the Father, the Son and the Holy Spirit,
now and forever and unto ages of ages. Amen.

Prayer from the Coptic liturgy

We rejoice with great joy
for the good news of the resurrection
of our Lord and Saviour Jesus Christ,
   who has been the fruit
   and the first-born of all who have fallen asleep;
   who destroyed the gates of hell,
   loosed the tyranny of death,
   and gave us the firm hope
   of the renewal of all human life.

Litany after the gospel, Armenian liturgy,
Office of Myrr-bearing Women

O God, you have spoken to us your divine and saving words.
Illumine the souls of us sinners
to comprehend that which has been read,
that we do not appear simply
   as hearers of your spiritual words,
   but doers of good deeds,
   true pursuers of faith,
   having a blameless life
   and a conduct without reproach
in Christ our Lord,
with whom you are blessed and glorified,
together with your all-holy and good, and life-giving Spirit,
now and forever and to the ages of ages.

Prayer from the liturgy of St James

Shine within our hearts, loving Master,
the pure light of your divine knowledge
and open the eyes of our minds
that we may comprehend the message of your gospel.
Instill in us, also, reverence for your blessed commandments,
so that having conquered sinful desires,
we may pursue a spiritual life,
thinking and doing all these things that are pleasing to you.

For you, Christ our God, are the light of our souls and bodies,
and to you we give glory
together with your Father who is without beginning
and your all holy Spirit, good and life giving Spirit,
now and forever and to the ages of ages. Amen.

Prayer from the liturgy of St John Chrysostom

Orthodox liturgy of Kiev

Romania

5. St John the Theologian.

Meditation: "You are the illumination of our souls and bodies, O Christ, our God..."

The illumination of our bodies? We can well understand that the light of the Word illumines our souls. But how and in what measure does he illumine our bodies? A few lines earlier the same prayer declared: "trampling down all carnal desires". Can the same flesh be both trampled down and illumined?

The flesh in itself is good, having been created and blessed by God. Wounded and weakened by the sin of our first parents, however, the flesh often becomes the origin of various temptations. It can become a wall of separation, an egocentric barrier, an instrument of struggle against the Spirit.

Those, however, are deviations. The flesh, such as God thought and purposed it, is an instrument of our salvation. It is in this sense that God is the principle of love between man and woman, making a sacrament of their conjugal union. For this reason, too, God obliges us to preserve our body and our physical health, as well as to pray for the sick. And God has exalted our flesh to such heights that he even assumed human flesh in the person of our Lord Jesus Christ.

It is for that reason that the liturgy, in the prayer before the reading of the gospel, can exhort us to "trample down" all desires of the flesh (those desires that are in themselves evil insofar as they separate us from God and from our sisters and brothers) while speaking at the same time of the "illumination of our bodies" as well as our souls.

From "Our Life in the Liturgy",
by a monk of the Eastern church, 20th century

Glory to You, O Lord, glory to You.

Thanksgiving

I bless you, O Lord.
Though I am powerless, you strengthen my weakness.
You stretch forth from above your helping hand
and bring me back unto yourself.
What shall I render to you, O all-good Master,
for all the good things you have done
and continue to do for me,
the sinner?
I will cease not to bless you all the days of my life,
my creator,
my benefactor
and my guardian.

Excerpt from a prayer to the Almighty God and Father
who loves humankind, St Basil the Great, 4th century

Lord, my God,
you are great, fearful and glorious,
the creator of every visible and spiritual creation,
you are faithful to your covenant and mercy,
for those who love you and keep your commandments,
I thank you both now and forever
for all the blessings,
seen and unseen,
that have been bestowed upon me.
Even up to this present time,
I praise, glorify and magnify you,
for everything

that has proven your rich mercy and compassion
to be wondrous in me,
helping me, out of your goodness and love for humankind,
from my mother's womb
and providing in every way
to protect and to govern in a holy manner
the matters of my life.

Excerpt from a daily prayer to our Lord Jesus Christ,
St John Chrysostom, 4th century

How many times, after I had sinned,
you comforted me, as a good father,
and you kissed me warmly as a son or a daughter,
and you stretched out your arms to me and cried out:
rise up, fear not, stand up, come!

Excerpt from a prayer to our Lord Jesus Christ,
St John of Damascus, 7th-8th century

O Master, Lord, God Almighty,
Father of our Lord, our God, our Saviour Jesus Christ,
we thank you upon every condition,
for any condition and in whatever condition.
For you have covered us,
supported us,
preserved us,
accepted us unto you,
had compassion on us,
sustained us
and brought us to this hour.
Therefore we pray and entreat your goodness,
O lover of humankind,
grant us to complete this holy day
and all the days of our life
in all peace with your fear. Amen.

Thanksgiving prayer, Coptic liturgy

Meditation: "Let our mouths be filled with praise, O Lord,
that we may celebrate your glory"! (Ps. 71:8)

We are not worthy, Lord, to offer you a hymn of praise
for the benefits you have vouchsafed to us,
but grant us this also by filling our mouths with praise;
and as you have given the grace of prayer to those who ask for it —
that we may know for what and how to pray —
so now give our lips the power to praise you.

A commentary on the divine liturgy,
St Nicholas Cabasilas, 14th century

Peace and Justice

Our spirit seeks you in the early dawn, O God,
for your commandments are light.
Teach us, O Master, your righteousness
and make us worthy to follow your commandments
with all our strength.
Take away from our hearts every darkness.
Grant to us the Sun of righteousness
and protect our lives from any bad influence
with the seal of your most Holy Spirit.
Direct our steps to the way of peace
and grant to us that this present morning may be peaceful
so that we may send up the morning hymns
to you the Father and the Son and the Holy Spirit,
the only God,
who is more than without beginning
and creator of all. Amen.

Excerpt from a morning prayer to the Holy Trinity,
St Basil the Great, 4th century

O Christ, our God,
author of life and giver of peace,
guide us
so that we may walk in your ways of righteousness
and arrive at the heaven of life and salvation in peace,
through your mercy.
For you are our helper and our deliverer
and to you is fitting glory,
dominion and honour,
now and for ever and unto the ages of ages. Amen.

Collect from the Armenian Sunrise Office

O Lord, rightly direct our goings in the ways of peace.
O Lord, direct and guide our souls
    and the souls of all the faithful
to walk on the way of righteousness
    and into life eternal. Amen.

Collect from the Armenian Sunrise Office

For peace let us pray to the Almighty God,
the Father of our Lord Jesus Christ,
    the king of peace,
that he may grant unto us yet many years of peace,
and may send unto us peace-loving authorities
to the glory and praise of his great and awesome name.
Let us also pray him to keep all peoples in peace
and to overthrow the foes who wage war upon us.

Evening prayer, ancient Armenian prayer book

Peace be with you, prophets,
peace be with you, apostles,
and peace be with you, martyrs,
who loved the Lord of peace;
and peace be with the holy church
in which dwell the sons and daughters of peace.

Vesper hymn, Syrian liturgy

Meditation: "Blessed are those who hunger and thirst after righteousness, for they shall be filled"

Jesus, answering in advance those who in our day accuse him of imposing on the poor by promising them consolation in another world, exclaims: "Blessed are those who hunger and thirst after righteousness" and therefore refuse to resign themselves to the suffering of others. In fact, it too often happens that a person, having reached maturity and having achieved a comfortable position in the world, will wish to maintain it by making various compromises with a society in which injustice reigns, saying: "It has always been like this," in order to justify himself or herself.

But blessed are those who maintain the purity of youth when everything seems clear and obvious and one is not afraid to confront those who subordinate truth and justice to individual or group interests or to reasons of state.

Blessed are those who, with Zola and Péguy, proclaimed the innocence of Dreyfus, condemned to penal servitude by the highest authority of the state! Blessed is Martin Luther King, who protested against the unjust oppression of African Americans and whose voice could not be silenced through assassination! Blessed is Pastor Niemöller, who with inflexible gentleness resisted Hitler's ferocity in the name of the gospel; and blessed is Solzhenitsyn, who stood up fearlessly against the Soviet Gulag. Blessed is Mother Teresa of Calcutta, who saves from death the starving children of India...

Of them all, the Lord says: "Blessed are those who hunger and thirst after righteousness, for they shall be satisfied." Unfortunately, some have thought that they could make God's justice reign at the point of the sword; but by making such an attempt, they have lost the kingdom of God within themselves. It is the cross — and not the crusade — which is the strongest weapon of the Christian in the fight for justice.

"The Living God, a Catechism
for the Christian Faith", 20th century

Matthew 5:3-11   Russian Orthodox hymn

Re - mem - ber your ser - vants, Lord,

when you come in your king - dom.

1. Bless - ed are the poor in spi - rit;

for theirs is the kingdom of hea - ven.

2. Bless - ed are those who mourn;

for they shall be com - fort - ed. 3. Bless - ed are the meek;

for they shall in - her - it the earth.

4. Bless - ed are those who hunger and thirst af - ter right-eous-ness;

for they shall be sat - is - fied.

5. Bless - ed are the mer - ci - ful;

for they shall ob - tain mer - cy.

6. Bless - ed are the pure in heart;

for they shall see God.

7. Bless - ed are the peace - ma - kers;

for they shall be called the chil - dren of God.

8. Bless - ed are those who are perse - cut - ed for right - eous - ness sake;

for theirs is the kingdom of hea - ven.

9. Bless - ed are you when the world re - viles you and per - se - cutes you;

and   utters all manner of   evil against you   false-ly   for my sake;

Re - joice   and   be   ex - ceed - ing   glad;

for great   is your reward in   hea   -   ven.

Re - mem - ber   your   ser - vants, Lord,

when   you come in your   king   -   dom.

6. Sts Xeni, Philothei, Makrina and Isidora.

The Struggle of the Martyrs, Saints and Confessors

To you, O Lord, great sower of creation,
the world offers the first-fruits of nature:
the God-bearing martyrs.
Through their intercessions,
and the intercessions of the Theotokos,
most merciful God,
keep your church in abiding peace. Amen.

Hymn, Feast of All Saints

O Christ, our God,
your church,
crimson with the blood of your martyrs all over the world,
as with a cloak of murex and porphyry,
cries out to you:
"Send your mercy upon your people,
grant peace to your fold,
and extend your great compassion upon our souls."

Hymn

O victorious martyrs of the Lord,
blessed is the earth
that received your blood,
and holy are the heavenly places
that opened to your souls!
You have vanquished the enemy in battle
and proclaimed Christ with courage.
We beg you to intercede with him,
the all-good one,
that he may save our souls.

Hymn

O beloved martyrs and habitations of the Spirit of truth,
who did conquer by the Spirit your desires and passions;
intercede with the Lord for the children of the church.

Matins hymn, Armenian Sunrise Office

The angels in heaven are glad for the sufferings of the martyrs,
and the creatures on earth wonder at the victory of the saints.
Having fought the great battle and having shown their virtue,
they were crowned by Christ.
The catholic church rejoices
and the faithful exult and cry out saying:
"Glory to you, O God."

Mid-day hymn, Armenian liturgy

Meditation: Ethics of the Resurrection

Mortality and death make struggle for survival inevitable, and create conditions for a Darwinian world, where the fittest survive, but only at the expense of the weakest. Death is the enemy from which one seeks security, and in the fallen world there is no other security than the means of the world: money, power, competitions, often violence — the ingredients of sinfulness. All these are unavoidable until death is vanquished with all the impulses for a worldly struggle for survival.

In the world, the struggle is actually hopeless, because death can only be postponed, not ultimately suppressed. The ultimate victory is that of Christ, a victory that is the Christian "good news" and the foundation of our hope. The "life in Christ" that begins at baptism is a life free from death. The Christian martyrs were venerated from the beginnings of Christianity; by their deaths they witnessed to this new life, just as the apostles, who had seen the risen Jesus with their own eyes. Christians, therefore, need not struggle for survival. Since they have life in themselves, they have the power to give, to serve, to live for others, without being concerned for their own survival interests.

Christian ethics is not a voluntary obligation; it is the manifestation of true life, an ethics of the resurrection.

"Humanity: Old and New", Fr John Meyendorff

7. *The resurrection.*

Orthodox liturgy

Russia

My soul mag - ni - fies the Lord,

and my spir - it re - joic - es in God my Sav - ior.

More hon'ra - ble than the Che - ru - bim,

and more glor - ious be - yond com - pare than the Ser - a - phim,

with - out stain you bore the Word of God,

and are tru - ly the Mo - ther of God, we mag - ni - fy you.

For He re - gard - ed the low - li - ness of His hand - maid;

for be-hold, from now all gen - er - a - tions shall call me bless-ed.

More   hon'ra - ble   than   the   Che - ru - bim...

For He   that is might - y mag - ni - fied me,

and Ho - ly is His name;

His mer - cy is on those who fear Him

and has sent the rich a - way, emp - ty.

More hon'ra - ble than the Che - ru - bim...

He has helped His ser - vant Is - ra - el,

in re - mem - brance of His mer - cy,

as He spoke to our fa - thers,

to Ab - ra - ham and to his pos - ter - i - ty for - ev - er.

More hon'ra - ble than the Che - ru - bim...

Creation

You, hills and mountains,
you, plains and valleys,
you, rivers and all creation,
    magnify your Lord
    who comes for our sake to be born.

Hymn, pre-feast of the nativity

Lord, Jesus Christ, our God,
who blessed the five loaves in the wilderness,
from which five thousand were fed,
bless also these loaves, this oil, this wine,
and all the fruits of the earth;
multiply them in this city, in this country,
and everywhere in your world;
sanctify your faithful who will receive them.
For you are the one who blesses
and feeds and sanctifies all creation,
O Christ our God,
and to you we give glory,
together with your eternal Father
and your all-holy, good and life creating Spirit,
now and ever and unto ages of ages. Amen

Blessing of bread

Praise the Lord, all works of the Lord.
Praise the Lord, you heavens, you angels of the Lord.
Praise the Lord, all waters above the heaven.

Praise the Lord, all powers.
Praise the Lord, sun and moon, stars of heaven.
Praise the Lord, all rain and dew, all winds.
   Praise the Lord, sing and exalt him
   throughout all the ages.

Praise the Lord, fire and heat,
   cold and summer heat,
   dews and snows.
Praise the Lord, nights and days, light and darkness.
Praise the Lord, ice and cold, frosts and snows.
Praise the Lord, lightnings and clouds.
   Praise the Lord, sing and exalt him
   throughout all the ages.

Let the earth bless the Lord.
Praise the Lord, mountains and hills,
   all things that grow on the earth.
Praise the Lord, you springs, seas and rivers.
Praise the Lord, you whales
   and all creatures that move in the waters.
Praise the Lord, all birds of the air, all beasts and cattle.
   Praise the Lord, sing and exalt him
   throughout all the ages.

Praise the Lord, you sons and daughters of men.
Praise the Lord, O Israel.
Praise the Lord, you priests of the Lord.
Praise the Lord, you servants of the Lord.
Praise the Lord, spirits and souls of the righteous.
Praise the Lord, you who are holy and humble in heart.
Praise the Lord, Ananiah, Azariah and Mishael.
Praise the Lord, apostles, prophets and martyrs of the Lord.
   We praise the Father, the Son
   and the Holy Spirit.
   Now and ever, and unto ages of ages. Amen.

We praise, bless and worship the Lord,
singing and exalting him
throughout the ages.

> Vesper hymn, holy Saturday, from the Hymn of the Three Youth
> in the Book of Daniel according to the Septuagint

Verse: If you, O Lord, should mark iniquities, Lord who could
       stand? For with you there is forgiveness (Ps. 129:3).

O Christ,
who brought all things into existence from nothing,
and with ineffable wisdom
gave to each one to accomplish unerringly
the goal which you laid down in the beginning,
O Saviour, Lover of humankind, as you are powerful,
bless the whole creation which you fashioned.

Verse: For your name's sake I have waited for you, O Lord; my soul
       has waited for your word, my soul has hoped in the Lord (Ps.
       129:5).

Give peace to all the nations, Lord,
and understanding in all things,
so that we may lead our life in tranquillity
and always keep the laws
which you laid down for all creation
for the unalterable maintenance
and government of the universe.

Verse: From the watch of dawn until the night, from the watch of
       dawn, let Israel hope in the Lord (Ps.129:6).

Lover of humankind,
keep unharmed the environment that clothes the earth,
through which, by your will,
we who inhabit the earth live
and move and have our being,
that we, your unworthy suppliants,
may be delivered from destruction and ruin.

Verse: For with the Lord there is mercy, and with him abundant
       redemption, and he will redeem Israel from all his iniquities
       (Ps. 129:7).

Fence round the whole creation, Christ Saviour,
with the mighty strength of your love for humankind,
and deliver the earth we inhabit
from the corruption which threatens it;
for we, your servants, have set our hopes on you.

Verse: Praise the Lord all nations! extol him all peoples (Ps. 116)!

Put an end, O Saviour, to the evil designs
which are being devised against us by senseless intent,
and turn aside from the earth every
destructive action of the works of human hands
which contrive corruption leading to perdition.

Verse: For great is his mercy to us, and the truth of the Lord
        endures for ever (Ps. 116).

O Lord, who wraps creation in clouds,
as godly David sang,
watch over the environment of the earth,
which you created from the beginning
for the preservation of mortals,
and give us the breath of the winds
and the flow of waters.

> Hymns, Office of Supplication for the Environment
> and for the Whole Creation, 20th century

Great are you, O Lord,
and wondrous are your works,
and no word will suffice to sing your wonders.
For you by your will
have out of nothingness brought all things into being
and by your power sustain all creation,
and by your providence direct the world.
You from the four elements have formed creation
and have crowned the cycle of the year with the four seasons.

All the spiritual powers tremble before you;
the sun praises you; the moon glorifies you;
the stars in their courses meet with you;
the light hearkens unto you;
the depths shudder at your presence;
the springs of water serve you.
You have stretched out the heavens as a curtain;
you have founded the earth upon the waters;
you have bounded the sea with sand;
you have poured forth the air for breathing;
the angelic powers minister unto you.
The cherubim and the seraphim,
as they stand and fly around you,
veil themselves with fear of your unapproachable glory.
For you,
being boundless and beginningless and unutterable,
came down on earth,
taking the form of a servant,
being made in human likeness.
For you, O Master, through the tenderness of your mercy,
could not endure the human race tormented by the devil,
but you came and saved us.
We confess your grace;
we proclaim your beneficence;
we do not hide your mercy.
You have set free our mortal nature.
All creation sings praises to you
who have revealed yourselves.
For you, our God, have appeared upon earth
and have dwelt among us.
You have sanctified the Jordan streams...

Excerpt from the Great Blessing of Water

Russia

Not strict ♩= 96

When you, O Lord, were bap-tized in the Jor - dan,

the wor - ship of the Trin - i - ty was made man - i - fest.

For the voice of the Fa- ther bore wit-ness un - to you,

call - ing you the be - lov - ed Son,

and the Spir - it in the form of a dove

con - firmed his word as sure and stead - fast.

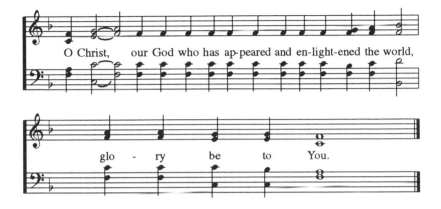

O Christ, our God who has ap-peared and en-light-ened the world,

glo - ry be to You.

Meditation: The Blessing of the Water

In the Orthodox feast of the Baptism of our Lord, the Feast of the Epiphany (which is sharply distinguished from the Western Christian Feast of the Epiphany, which celebrates the visit of the Magi to the newly born Christ-child), creation is perceived as participating in Christ's saving work. The baptism of Christ in water is an important aspect of the hymnology of the day. The water takes on a representational character, a symbol of the material created world. The incarnate Son of God is immersed in it. Water becomes a vehicle for saving and sanctifying acts. As a symbol and representative element of the created world, it intimately shares in the salvation of the world.

While there is of course a distinction between the spiritual and material worlds, there is no sharp separation, much less a harsh contradiction. The salvation of the world, though primarily for the sake of humanity, precisely because the human being is a microcosm, is redemption for the material world as well. The spiritual and the material form one reality, God's creation. In the sacrament-like blessing of the water, it is perceived as becoming an agent of sanctification. The church thus prays: "Grant to all those who touch it, who anoint themselves with it or drink from it, sanctification, blessing, cleansing and health."

"The Integrity of Creation: Ethical Issues",
Fr Stanley Harakas

Healing

O Lord Almighty,
the healer of our souls and bodies,
   you put down and raise up,
   you chastise and heal also;
visit now in your great mercy
our brothers and sisters who are sick.
Stretch forth your hand that is full of healing and health,
   and get them up from their bed,
   and cure them of their illness.
Put away from them the spirit of disease and of every malady,
   pain and fever to which they are bound;
and if they have sins and transgressions,
   grant to them remission and forgiveness,
   since you love all your people.
Yes, Lord my God,
pity your creation,
through the compassion of your only-begotten Son,
together with your all-holy, good and life-creating Spirit,
with whom you are blessed,
both now and ever, and to the ages of ages. Amen.

Prayer for the sick

Lord,
it was not the pool
that healed the paralytic, but your word.
The power of your voice
   was stronger than the chronic bond of the disease.

Therefore he cast away the burden of sickness
   and took up his bed
   as a witness to your abundant mercies.
Lord, glory to you!

Hymn of praises, Sunday of the paralytic

O Lord our God,
who by word alone healed all diseases,
who cured the kinswoman of Peter,
you chastise with pity and heal according to your goodness;
you are able to put aside every malady and infirmity,
you are the same Lord,
grant aid to your servants
and cure them of every sickness which grieves them;
lift them up from their bed of pain,
send down upon them your great mercy,
and if it be your will,
give to them health and a complete recovery;
for you are the physician of our souls and bodies,
and to you we offer glory:
to the Father, and to the Son, and to the Holy Spirit,
both now and ever, and to the ages of ages. Amen.

Prayer for the sick

O Christ, who alone are our defender,
visit and heal your suffering servants
delivering them from sickness and grievous pains.
Raise them up
   that they may sing to you
   and praise you without ceasing;
through the prayers of the Theotokos,
O you who alone loves humankind.

Prayer for the sick

*8. The healing of the paralytic, and the resurrection of Lazarus,
from a Bible dated 1362.*

Meditation: The Healing of the Leper

The leper... lamented in a flood of tears;
Every hour he would notice that he took on some additional pain,
and he says words such as these:
"... I have not a single hope of health
unless Christ will give it to me,
the lover of humankind.
In haste, then, my soul, go to Christ the Son of the Virgin,
in order that he may give the healing
which from human hands it was not possible to receive.
Christ gave the man who was blind and in darkness from birth
the sight of which nature had deprived him.
He snatched from death the son of the widow;
he strengthened the ancient limbs of the paralytic,
which had been enervated through disease.
Nothing stands up against him
as God and Creator.
Therefore I have faith that he is not merely son of man,
the lover of humankind."

On the Healing of the Leper,
St Romanos the Melodist, 6th century

Unity

Benefactor,
King of the ages,
and Creator of all creation,
receive your church which approaches you through your Christ.
To each grant what is useful.
Lead us all to perfection
and render us worthy of your sanctifying grace
bringing us together
in your holy, catholic and apostolic church,
adorned with the precious blood of your only-begotten Son,
our Lord and Saviour Jesus Christ,
with whom you are blessed and glorified,
together with your all-holy, good and life-giving Spirit,
now and forever and to the ages of ages. Amen.

Prayer from the liturgy of St James

O God, Master of all, and loving God,
unworthy though we are,
make us worthy at this hour
that, cleansed of all deceit and hypocrisy,
we may be united with one another
in the bond of peace and love,
being established in the sanctification of your divine knowledge
through your only-begotten Son
with whom you are blessed,
together with your all-holy, good and life-giving Spirit,
now and forever and to the ages of ages. Amen.

Prayer from the liturgy of St James

Master and Lord Almighty,
look down from heaven upon your church,
upon all your people, and upon all your flocks,
and save all of us, your unworthy servants,
the creatures of your fold;
grant to us your peace, your love and your help;
send down upon us the gifts of your most Holy Spirit,
that in a pure heart and with a good conscience
we may salute one another with a holy kiss,
not in hypocrisy, but blameless and unspotted,
in one spirit, in the bond of peace and of love,
one body and one spirit, in one faith,
as we have also been called in one hope of our calling,
that we may all of us arrive
at the divine and boundless affection,
in Christ Jesus, our Lord,
with whom you are blessed. Amen.

Prayer from the liturgy of St Mark

Meditation: Prayer for Unity

Unity as union is not only revealed by God in Christ, but is also realized among people through his Spirit. The essence of this union is a new life for humankind in full communion with each other through and because of the real presence of God in history. We must, therefore, continuously remind ourselves that this given fact of unity has led us to a difficult process of growth towards perfect unity in Christ. It is in this context alone that we are able to understand St Paul's references to the unity of the church. On the one hand, he refers to the given historical fact, which makes us partakers of an already established oneness, being "built upon the foundation of the apostles and prophets" (Eph. 2:20). And on the other hand, he is calling us to concern for "building up the body of Christ, until we all attain to the unity of the faith and of the knowledge of the Son of God, to maturity, to the measure of the stature of the fullness of Christ" (Eph 4:12-13).

The Eastern tradition bases its own conceptions and continuous prayer for unity on this apparent dualism: on the one hand to be supported by this unity, on the other hand to have a vocation for this unity. There is a double relationship between the overwhelming grace of God and the weak and sinful acts of men and women.

"The Witness and the Service of Eastern Orthodoxy
to the One Undivided Church", Nikos Nissiotis

Litanies

Have mercy upon us, O God, according to your great mercy; we pray
you, hear and have mercy.
Kyrie, eleison.

as taught by Metropolitan Mar Gregorios Yohanna Ibrahim: Syria

Kyrie eleison in Aramaic

Again we pray for all those responsible for our churches and com-
munities, and for all brothers and sisters in Christ, for every Christian
soul afflicted and weary, in need of God's mercies and help.
Kyrie, eleison.

Again we pray for the protection of this city and those who dwell in it; for the peace of the whole world; for the well-being of the holy churches of God; for the servants of God here present and all those working for the ecumenical movement.
Kyrie, eleison.

Again we pray for the salvation and help of all who labour and serve; for those who travel; for the healing of the sick; for the deliverance of captives and refugees.
Kyrie, eleison.

Again we pray for the repose, refreshment and blessed memory of and forgiveness of sins of all who have gone to rest before and lie here and everywhere.
Kyrie, eleison.

Again we pray that God will keep this city and every city and country from famine, pestilence, earthquake, flood, fire, pollution, war and civil strife, that our good God who loves humanity will be gracious and merciful and deliver us from his righteous chastisement which impends against us, and have mercy on us.
Kyrie, eleison.

Again we pray that the Lord God will hear the prayer of us sinners and have mercy on us.
Kyrie, eleison.

Hear us, O God our Saviour, the hope of all the ends of the earth, and of those who are far off upon the sea; and be gracious, be gracious, O Master, unto us sinners and have mercy on us. For you are a merciful God who loves humanity and all your creation, and unto you we give glory, to the Father, and to the Son, and to the Holy Spirit, now and ever and unto ages of ages.
Amen.

                                                    Vespers, Breaking of Bread

Let us be attentive and devoted.
In peace let us pray to the Lord.
Lord, have mercy (the same after each petition).

Mt. Athos Melody: Greece

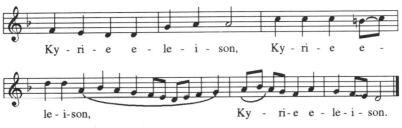

Ky - ri - e e - le - i - son, Ky - ri - e e -
le - i - son, Ky - ri - e e - le - i - son.

Lord, have mercy.

For the peace of God and his loving kindness towards humanity, and the salvation of our souls, let us pray to the Lord.

For peace in the whole world and unity among all the holy churches of God, let us pray to the Lord.

For this city, every city and town and for those who dwell in them in faith and in reverence of God, and for their peace and security, let us pray to the Lord.

For those in captivity and exile, for our brothers and sisters in cruel slavery and for their return to their own peace and joy, let us pray to the Lord.

For every Christian soul in affliction and suffering, needing God's mercy and help; for the return of those who have been led astray; for the health of those ill; for the rescue of those in captivity, let us pray to the Lord.

For those who bear fruit and do good work in God's holy churches, for those who remember the poor, the widows, the orphans, the strangers and the needy; and for those who have charged us to remember them in our prayers, let us pray to the Lord.

For our prayer, that it may be heard and be well accepted by God and that his mercies and compassion be sent to us, let us pray to the Lord.

Liturgy of St James

Pray for the rising of the rivers' waters this year, that Christ our Lord may bless it and raise it to its measure, grant a cheerful touch unto the lands, support the human beings, save the cattle and forgive us our sins.
Lord, have mercy.

Arabic   Orthodox

Ya Rab   ur-ham. Ya Rab   ur - ham. Ya Rab   ur-ham.

Kyrie eleison . Lord have mercy on us.

Pray for the trees, vegetation and the planting of the land this year, that Christ our Lord may bless them to grow and bring forth plentiful fruit, have compassion upon his creation and forgive us our sins.
Lord, have mercy.

Pray for the winds, the crops, the vine and every fruit-bearing tree in the whole world, that Christ our Lord may bless them, to reach harvesting without harm and forgive us our sins.
Lord, have mercy.

Accord, O Lord, a cheerful touch to the earth, water it and dispose our life as you deem fit. Crown this year with your goodness, for the sake of the poor of your people, the widow, the orphan, the stranger and for our sake. For our eyes are focused upon you, our hope, and seek your holy name. You provide us our food in due course. Deal with us, O Lord, according to your goodness, you, the feeder of everybody. Fill our hearts with joy and grace, so that, as we always have sufficiently of all things, we may grow in every good deed.
Amen.

Coptic liturgy

Remember, Lord, the dew of the air and the fruits of the earth, bless them and keep them without loss.
Kyrie, eleison.

Russia

Ky - ri - e   e - lei - son,   Ky - ri - e   e   lei - son,
Gos - po-di   po-mi - lui.   Gos - po - di   po - mi - lui.

Ky - ri - e   e - lei   -   i - son.
Gos - po - di   po-mi   -   lui

Remember, Lord, the coming down of the rains and the waters and the rivers, and bless them.

Remember, Lord, the plants and the seeds and the fruits of the fields of every year, bless them and make them abundant.

Remember, Lord, the safety of your own holy church.

Remember, Lord, the sick among your people, visit them in your mercy and heal them in your compassion.

Remember, Lord, the captives of your people, and bring them again in peace to their dwelling places.

Remember, Lord, the afflicted and distressed.

Remember, Lord, your servants, the poor who are under oppression. Through your only begotten Son, our Lord and our God and our Saviour Jesus Christ, through whom to you, with him and with the Holy Spirit, be glory and dominion both now and ever. Amen.

Ethiopian liturgy

Meditation: Lord, Have Mercy!

Why is it that, whereas the priest asks them to pray for so many different things, the faithful in fact ask for one thing only — mercy? Why is this the sole cry they send forth to God?

In the first place, it is because this prayer implies both gratitude and confession. Secondly, to beg God's mercy is to ask for his kingdom, that kingdom which Christ promised to give to those who seek for it, assuring them that all things else of which they have need will be added unto them (Matt. 6:33). Because of this, this prayer is sufficient for the faithful, since its application is general.

How do we know that the kingdom of God is signified by his mercy? In this way: Christ, speaking of the reward of the merciful, and of the recompense of kindness which they will receive from him, in one place says that they shall obtain mercy, and in another that they shall inherit the kingdom; thus proving that God's mercy and the inheritance of the kingdom are one and the same thing.

A commentary on the divine liturgy,
St Nicholas Cabasilas, 14th century

Romania

Doam - ne   mi - lu - ie - ste.

Doam - ne   mi - lu - ie - ste.

Kyrie eleison, Lord have mercy.

Peter Dinev: Bulgaria

Gos - po - di po - mi - luj.

Gos - po - di po - mi - luj.

Gos - po - di po - mi - luj.

Gos - po - di po - mi - luj.

Gos - po - di po - mi - luj.

Gos - po - di po - mi - luj.

Te - be Gos - po - di.

A min.

Kyrie eleison.

Kyrie eleison.

Liturgical Resources

The Book of Common Prayer of the Syrian Church, transl. by Bede Griffiths, ed. Jacob Vellian, Kerala, vol. 3, 1973.

A Collection of Prayers from the Ancient Armenian Book of Offices and Divine Liturgy, ed. Tarenig Poladian, Calcutta, Mullick Press, 1958.

Divine Liturgy of the Armenian Apostolic Orthodox Church, with Variables, Complete Rubrics and Commentary, transl. Archbishop Tiran Nersoyan, London, Saint Sarkis Church, rev. 5th ed. 1984.

Divine Liturgy of the Armenian Church, New York, Diocese of the Armenian Church of America, 5th ed. 1982.

The Divine Liturgy of St James, Brother of the Lord, a new transl. by members of the faculty of Hellenic College, Holy Cross Greek Orthodox School of Theology, Brookline MA, Holy Cross Orthodox Press, 1988.

The Divine Liturgy of St John Chrysostom, a new transl. by members of the faculty of Hellenic College, Holy Cross Greek Orthodox School of Theology, Brookline MA, Holy Cross Orthodox Press, 1985.

Eastern Christian Liturgies, ed. Peter D. Day, Shannon, Irish Univ. Press, 1972.

The Liturgies of St Mark, St James, St Clement, St Chrysostom and the Church of Malabar, transl. J.M. Neale, New York, AMS Press, 1969.

Liturgy of the Ethiopian Orthodox Church (Extracts), transl. Marcus Daoud, Addis Ababa, 1959.

A Manual of Eastern Orthodox Prayers, London, SPCK-Fellowship of SS Alban and Sergius, 1945.

An Orthodox Prayer Book, transl. John von Holzhausen and Michael Gelsinger, ed. N.M. Vaporis, Brookline MA, Holy Cross Orthodox Press, 1977.

The Sunrise Office of the Armenian Church, transl. Archbishop Tiran Nersoyan, New York, Diocese of the Armenian Church of America, 1969.

Voices in the Wilderness, An Anthology of Patristic Prayers, ed. and transl. from the Greek by N.S. Hatzinikolaou, Brookline MA, Holy Cross Orthodox Press, 1988.

Nicholas Cabasilas, *A Commentary on the Divine Liturgy*, transl. J.M. Hussey and P.A. McNulty, London, SPCK, 1960.

St Symeon of Thessalonike, Treatise on Prayer — an Explanation of the Services Conducted in the Orthodox Church, transl. H.L.N. Simmons, Brookline MA, Hellenic College Press, 1984.

Theodore Stylianopoulos, *A Year of the Lord, Liturgical Bible Studies*, Brookline MA, Greek Orthodox Archdiocese, Department of Religious Education, vols 1-4, 1981-85.